Made in United States
Orlando, FL
01 December 2023

39956562R00065